SAND DUNES

Purge

ABOUT THE AUTHOR

S Mahadevan Thampy is among the best known names in current Malayalam fiction. An acclaimed novelist and short story writer, he is known for his deep and incisive analyses of social issues with a personal touch. His novels on Kashmir and Sri Lanka are testaments to the immeasurable beauty of empathy and creativity of the author; not just that, immaculate research and domain knowledge keep these works grounded and relatable to the common man. Thampy has already published more than ten works of fiction. His love and care for human beings and the environment in which they live suffuse every sentence he writes. Most of his novels have been serialized in premier literary magazines in Malayalam and translated into other languages including Tamil, Kannada and Hindi. His major works include Azadi (in english), Sisirathile Suryan (The Winter Sun), Ente Neelasumudram (My Blue Sea), Athirukal & Adhinivesham (Borders & Invasions). 'Purge' is the English translation of his Malayalam novel 'Alakalillatha Kadal' originally published in 2008. A much awarded author, Thampy began his career as a journalist, after graduating in Economics and Journalism from the Delhi University. Later, he joined the Kerala government service and went on to become an Additional Director with the Information and Public Relations Department and he now serves as a media consultant.

Purge

A novel about the unknown victims
of the of Sri Lankan war victims

Mahadevan Thampi

Translated from Malayalam by
P. Muraleedharan

SAND DUNES

SAND DUNES

SAND DUNES is an imprint of the Green Books

Green Books
India

www.greenbooksindia.com

ISBN : 978 93 89671 64 3

First Impression 2020

Purge

April 20, 2008
Sunday

A flaming water column!

Originating from the depths of the sea and sweeping aside the waves, it creates countless droplets of water. Beneath those spherical particles, the silhouette of a tall and muscular man emerges. There is a sword in his right hand; the index finger of his left hand is pointing at someone. In a flash, that sword rises in the sky and comes down with tremendous power... I was stunned. Suddenly I got back to my senses, and opened my eyes.

It was the sixth time I was having this weird dream. The first time I had it was at the Le-Pang base, where I dozed off for a while, while waiting for the army's helicopter. Next time, it was during a trip to Leh and on my visits to Srinagar and New Delhi when I was so tired that my eyes closed on their own.

It was already ten in the morning and I was still in a peculiar stage between sleep and drowsiness. I was on a flight from Delhi to Chennai, and had this disturbing dream twice and woke up abruptly during the journey. So, I kept awake during my journey from Chennai to Madurai and I travelled to Munnamsathiram via Rameswaram by car. I got scared of the recurring dream that chased me wherever I went that I kept my eyelids open despite being very tired.

My destination was Arichal Munai, I needed to reach there by eight at night. The road led only up to Munnamsathiram, and from there I had to cross Dhanushkodi to reach Arichal Munai, which was a stretch of land jutting into the sea, with no human habitation. A boat was waiting there to take us to Sri Lanka.

Valliyur Vasan was waiting at Munnamsathiram with his sea van to take us to Arichal Munai, a place having no roads.

Vasan needs a brief introduction here. Vasan and his two aides controlled all the cargo movements, including the illegal boat services, between the Indian and Sri Lankan coasts. The trio smuggled essential commodities like rice, kerosene, diesel and medicines to Sri Lanka. Vasan, who was born in Valliyur village located between Nagercoil and Tirunelveli, considered to be the undisputed king of land and sea that stretched between Arichal Munai and Kadalur. The others in the trio were Swan Rabeer and Dhammika Pereira.

While Swan Rabeer, an Indonesian based at Kankesanthurai, managed their operations in the sea, Dhammika Pereira, a Sri Lankan from Trincomalee, was in charge of the Sri Lankan coast. Though they professed that their main occupation was to smuggle kerosene, diesel, rice and medicines into Lanka illegally, it was believed that they were also engaged in transporting arms and ammunition for the Liberation Tigers of Tamil Eelam (LTTE) and arranging training for them in foreign countries.

Some time ago, I happened to see a large quantity of rifles and engines of high-speed motor bikes in their boat.

Seeing Vasan at Munnamsathiram, my colleague Cicil Glancer, the international affairs editor of View TV, heaved a sigh of relief and looked cheerful for the first time in our journey. She was glued to her laptop throughout the journey and seemed to be in an apprehensive mood.

I knew that her father Glancer, a media baron and a business tycoon based in Norway, had a good relationship with Vasan. He was also Vasan's saviour in several occasions even when he was caught red-handed with arms and ammunition in international waters. Once Glancer had managed to send him back to Sri Lanka hours after Vasan was caught with a ship laden with arms.

No wonder, Vasan and Cicil shared a father-daughter relationship. A polyglot and an expert in handling modern day communication gadgets, she was on a special assignment in South Asia. Her on the field reporting of Afghanistan war had hogged headlines worldwide, and made her a celebrity among the journalist community.

She had surprised the world with her Afghan war footages, which were taken without a camera. Her mysterious skills at photography were still a topic of discussion in the media world.

But she chose to share a well-kept secret with me. I had never seen her without a pair of goggles kept hooked to a thick platinum chain around her neck and they were not ordinary at all. Her specs were a specam, a smart device which could record sounds and visuals and whenever she felt the need to record something, she used to put it on her face. A fully-charged specam could record continuously for 240 hours.

The specialty of the glasses was that it could take photos even in pitch dark situations. The unique camera of the specs, which cost her around $3 million, was specially designed by a NASA scientist who made cameras for spaceships. She frequented conflict zones with these unique spectacles, and earned the label of a mysterious journalist who could do the impossible.

Being a correspondent in charge of the region, I was asked to join her mission when she reached Sri Lanka after covering her assignments in Myanmar, Bangladesh, Nepal and Pakistan. She received an unusual message on her satellite phone from her father when we were speaking to Indian Defence officers at Le-pang at around 2 A.M.

This was the message: "Both of you should reach Chinnatheevu on Indo-Lanka sea route tonight. A big surprise is waiting there for you. Let us show it to the world before anyone else..."

The sender of this message was none other than her father Glancer. He might have got some tip off about some newsworthy development in the area. He might have received the information from satellite pictures, or Tigers or even from the Sri Lankan forces. It could also be from a reliable source looking for an exclusive breaking news.

As I felt the need to report it faithfully, I asked her to seek more details from her father. I made her ask him whether it was about the exodus of refugees to India. He refused to divulge more, but said what we were going to find would shock the world. He assured us that he had made all the arrangements for our special assignment.

As it was an official invitation, we managed to find an army helicopter to reach our destination in that cold, wee hours. We reached Arichal Munai after a tiring flight, lasting hours; we had no idea that we were about to face an awkward situation there. A frail woman, past her middle age, had both I and Cicil completely shaken.

We found her hiding near the boat in waist-deep water, carrying a long walking stick in her arms and a rucksack on her shoulders.

Vasan was waiting for the wind to subside and start our voyage after midnight, which according to him was the ideal time for our requirement. He asked us to have our dinner and rest in the boat itself.

Leaving us in the boat along with boat driver Saravanan, Vasan left for the other side of the beach for something or the other. Surprising us, the woman came out from her hiding place and introduced herself in English with a perfect Scottish accent.

She was Sathyamma, who had fled to Indian shores on a speed boat along with her three daughters and a son when the ethnic conflict escalated in Sri Lanka.

She said that either Tamil Tigers or the Sri Lankan Navy attacked their boat and kidnapped her three daughters along with a few fellow travellers. Sathyamma managed to reach the Indian shore on another boat, with the help of her son.

She was yet to recover from the tragedy that happened near Chinnatheevu. The assailants might have dumped them somewhere in Sri Lanka after satiating their lust. She said she could still hear her daughters crying out aloud "Amma, Amma". She wanted to see her daughters, dead or alive, and wanted us to allow her to accompany us.

The boat driver vehemently rejected her request, may be thinking that we might concede to her request to allow her to accompany us. He cautioned us: "You should not listen to this mad woman."

He paused for a while, looked at our eyes, and whispered to us as if he was sharing a top secret with us. "You know, she approaches all boats and makes the same request. But nobody has taken her words seriously as they know the truth."

However, she completely ignored the boat driver, and fixed her gaze on Cicil. Then she began speaking in a peculiar tone.

"The cries of a mother, who has had the misfortune of watching her boat destroyed in the high seas and her three daughters forcibly taken away by unknown men, to be killed or raped brutally, may sound mad at times. Those who are really humane would understand their pain."

She stopped and looked at us with eyes filled with hope and made a fervent appeal: "I see humane kindness in you. Please take me along with you..."

I was moved by the words of Sathyamma, suffused with an amazing purity and poignancy, that make one obey. In her appearance and behaviour, there was something that made us feel an extraordinary pull towards her.

Cicil got emotional and told me Sathyamma reminded

her of her own mother. She had lost her when she was hardly seven years old.

As a professional, she thought Sathyamma could help her in our hunt for the exclusive story her father wanted us to break for his channel. Her idea was to travel to the place of origin of Sri Lankan Tamils' exodus to India. Cicil said, "We can achieve our aim through Sathyamma."

I found her idea brilliant, and we said almost simultaneously, "Let's take her along."

The boat driver who might have overheard us, said in a harsh voice, "If this woman is coming, I'm not on. You can have some other person to operate the boat" and left.

The boat driver's words annoyed Cicil, who was very particular about seeing her decisions prevail at the end. She would do anything to make that happen.

"I am going to meet Vasan. Make no mistake, we'll be going to Sri Lanka with her. By the time I come back, you finish off your 'duty'." She told me.

By the word 'duty' she was taking a dig at my diary writing habit. Wherever I was, I would finish my diary writing by 12 a.m. by noting down all the things happened on that particular day.

As I guessed the day was going to be dramatic and hectic, I had already noted down the happenings when I got time. Half of my job was done during our trip, and when Cicil asked "to finish my daily duty," I was writing the last sentence in my diary under the spotlight of the boat.

My day began at the extreme north of our country, precisely at Le-pang at the Indo-China border in the majestic Himalayas. And my day was ending at the extreme south of India in a place called Arichal Munai, India, known as 'no man's land'. What a contrast! A journey starting from the extreme north and ending at the extreme south of India in the same day... It was my first of its kind of experience.

I looked at my watch. The time is 11.53 P.M.

April 21, 2008

Monday

"**A**re you a Malayalee?"

Sathyamma asked me while I was shutting the diary. It seemed she was waiting for me to put the diary down.

The moment I said "Yes", she threw me another question.

"Where are you from?"

"Thiruvananthapuram." I replied.

"Do you know there a place called Chinnachala?" She asked again.

A street lying parallel to the famous Chala market in Thiruvannanthapuram, Chinnachala is no longer there. A by-pass to Kilippalam has been built over it.

She did not wait for my reply and continued.

"My grandfather lived there. Our maternal ancestral home was also there."

"Who is your grandfather? What is the name of your ancestral home?" I asked her.

Her reply was immediate. "Kolappa Pillai. Our ancestral house is Pillaiveedu."

I was taken aback by her reply and tried my best not to reveal that in my expressions. To clarify my doubts, I asked her, "Your grandfather was Ceylon Pillai?"

She took a deep breath, and said with a smile, "Yes."

I dived in to my adolescent memories. For we, the children, Poilappillai was an interesting person. He used to visit my mother's eldest uncle (Karanavar, head of the joint family) Sathyavageeshwaran and offered lots of gifts at his feet every year during Onam. We were told that he was coming from the other side of the ocean, which added to our curiosity and we developed a great admiration for him. He used to bring sweets and special toys for us, which were not available in the local markets. Besides these items, he used to bring jappanam, a reputed variety of tobacco leaves from Jaffna, enough to last one full year, for our grand uncle.

The tobacco would be finely sliced after a thorough cleaning and mixed with jaggery and ghee by Pillai himself. He would add dried ginger, clove, cardamom and saffron to the mixture, stir it well and then store it in an air-tight container. The aroma that came out during the process was very lovely and it would waft over the whole area. We used to watch this 'magical' process with great interest and curiosity. Pillai was a dependent of our grand uncle, a powerful and very spiritual feudal chieftain.

Pillai had a business firm in the Chala market. It was heard that his marriage was not to his liking, but that he had to marry a woman from a Tamil family in Jaffna due to pressure from his family. After the marriage he settled down in Jaffna, but he made it a point to come and meet my grand uncle once in a year until his death.

He had great respect and love our grand uncle and was indebted to him. It is said that during a family dispute, his opponents had brought Chettys from Kutralam to kill Pillai. Our grand uncle jumped into their midst with a long sword, chased them away and saved Pillai's life.

In each of his visits, he used to narrate that incident like a sacred ritual. We were told that grand uncle gifted that sword to Poilapillai and told him to keep it with himself for his safety.

Whenever he came, he would stay in our house for about a month. During one such visit, he brought his wife and baby daughter. He placed the chubby child on our grand uncle's lap and asked him to name her after him. Such was his devotion and love for our uncle. But grand uncle refused his request saying it was a baby girl.

"This is my daughter and you should name her after you."

As Pillai was adamant, my grand uncle lifted the child close to his face and whispered into the baby's ear "Sathyamma".

"With this picture vivid in my mind, I asked her," Are you Sathyamma?"

With irrepressible happiness, she replied, "Yes, yes."

Thereafter she began to speak non-stop. "Sathyawageeshwaran was a god-like figure to my father, and I was named after him. My father died in Jaffna the same day he breathed his last at Rameshwaram."

I could not wait for long to reveal my identity. I told her, "He was my grand uncle. It was he who raised me; my initial 'S' stands for his name, Sathyavaageeshwaran."

The moment I said this, she raised her eyes to the sky, said, "Oh God, you are so kind! Would the tradition of magnanimity and valour continue? Would my family be blessed with a saviour in this generation as well?"

She waded through the water, and touched my hands. At the moment, I felt the touch of my grand uncle on my hands.

My grand uncle died at Rameshwaram during a pilgrimage and was cremated there. We grew up hearing that our grand uncle was specially blessed to have died at the sacred place. And Sathyamma formed part of that blessing.

On my insistence, Sathyamma narrated her life story. She had three brothers – Muthulingam, Nagalingam and Kumaralingam. Their whereabouts were not known ever since they joined LTTE.

She was married to Yogeeshwaran, a tea merchant, and they had four children, one son and three daughters.

When Yogeeshwaran was killed, she heard several rumours on his death: that the guerillas eliminated her husband for refusing to join LTTE and that the Sri Lankan army mistook him for an agent of Tigers and killed him.

Whatever might be the reason, his decomposed body was found at Jaffna exit point with his tongue cut. It was obvious that he had been brutally tortured before his death.

While narrating the horrific incident, Sathayamma sobbed uncontrollably. I also found it difficult to control my feelings, and felt as if my mother was crying before my eyes.

I made her sit in the boat, and to change the topic asked her, "Where is your son? You did not tell us anything about him."

Tears dripping down her cheeks, she told me curtly, "for heaven's sake, please don't ask anything about him."

It was not a request, but rather a command. So, I asked her about her three missing daughters.

"How old were your daughters? Were they married? Were they educated?"

"The eldest one is Savithri. She is twenty four. The second one is Saroja, aged twenty two and sixteen year old Sathyavathi is the youngest one. None of them are married. Schools have been closed for years in Jaffna, and therefore, they could not study."

"Then how did the family live? What did you do for a living? Why did you leave your home? What do you do here?"

She replied, "I had studied in a Scottish School. Though I did not go for work, I used to give English tuitions to children."

Before Sathyamma could complete her answers, Vasan was heard shouting. "Hey, Saravana, let's make a move."

Then he looked at me apologetically and said, "Don't take his words seriously. He is a new guy, joined us just a few weeks ago. He is getting accustomed to our way of doing things."

Saravanan came running from the darkness. He got into the boat and this time, he did not protest at all.

Vasan asked me secretly, "Are you taking her along

with you? Hope you have given it enough thought! Won't it affect your work?"

I replied firmly, "No, not at all." Cicil also supported me.

"Anyway, I am not feeling very comfortable about our journey. I have arranged one more boat to escort you. And it will be better if I come with you. I have made all the arrangements."

When Vasan said this, we agreed to his proposal. From then on, there was no delay. The boat moved towards the South splitting apart the waves. There was a strong wind blowing against us.

I looked at Sathyamma. She was sitting hunched in a corner of the boat with her hands tightly wrapped around a long stick which was almost equal to her height. She looked at us with great gratitude. When Cicil smiled at her with kindness and sympathy, her eyes seemed to be filled with radiance, brighter than the spotlight in the boat.

Vasan was busy adjusting the spotlight of the boat. Cicil had given Vasan a Ray Indicator she brought from

Norway, which could reduce the brightness of the spotlight. This was done to avoid any attacks on the boat.

The spotlight was adjusted in such a way that it would emit light equal to that 666 candle lights so that the Tigers and Sri Lankan Navy would mistake the boat for a Norwegian one. The Tigers did not consider Norway as an enemy; same was the case with the Sri Lankan Navy even though the government rejected the Norwegian offer of mediation. However, the Sri Lankan government maintained cordial diplomatic relations with Norway.

The boat moved very fast for almost an hour, and gradually it reduced speed and came to a standstill. Then Vasan said, "we have reached our destination." Cicil sharpened her ears and got up.

"Shall we wait at the island?" Vasan asked.

By the time our boat was anchored, the escort boat arrived.

While we were waiting for the escort boat to anchor, Vasan said, "Those who are fleeing to the Indian shores as refugees are mostly from the north-western region of Sri Lanka. The life there is miserable. No way one can lead a normal life over there. If they support the Tigers, police would arrest them; if they side with the police, the Tigers won't allow them to live. If they take a neutral stand, both the Tigers and the government forces would harass them and threaten them to make a choice between them. Keep aside the problems of adults; the children, especially girls, cannot survive out there at all. That is why this exodus."

Vasan continued. "The refugees are mostly from places like Jaffna, Mannar, Mullaitheevu and Kilinochi. They travel at night in speedboats and try to give the slip to the Tigers and the Sri Lankan Navy. The boat operators charge anywhere between Rs 5,000 to Rs 8,000 per person. The boats start the journey after midnight and reach Arichal Munai early in the morning. In case they are spotted by the Sri Lankan Navy, they will kill them or put them behind bars. The situation is not different if they are caught by the Tigers. Nobody knows the statistics of the people caught like during their frantic attempts to escape to the Indian shores."

In half-an-hour, we saw three boats rushing towards us from the South with two small ships chasing them.

What followed was intermittent gunshots and screams of people. Cicil watched all these things through her specam and recorded them. Sathyamma became tense and tried to scream, Vasan shut her mouth with his hands for a few minutes.

The firing and the cries might have continued for 10 minutes. Two of the three boats we saw were completely destroyed. No one knew what happened to the people in those boats. The third boat sped away at lightning speed towards the North. The ships left the scene after half an hour. But Cicil could record everything in her specam.

Sathyamma murmured: "This was what happened to us also."

Vasan replied in low tones, "It is Sri Lankan Navy, and the ships belong to them."

Cicil wanted to go to the spot where the action took place.

The first scene we saw under the spotlight was that of a woman's corpse floating on water. She was holding her infant close to her chest with her left hand; on taking a close look, we saw that she was holding on to a boy with her right hand. A feeding bottle, a trunk, three plastic buckets and a floor mat were seen undulating on the waves. A little further, the dead body of a pet dog, shot in its head, still in chains. Kitchen utensils, aluminum pots, plates and other household items. We also saw three other dead bodies floating face down in the ocean. All the bodies bore bullet marks.

Our boat moved very slowly.

Debris of two speed boats were strewn over the water surface in a radius of one kilo metre. We counted 18 dead bodies – nine women, six children and three men. All the men were in their old age. We also spotted the carcasses of a dog and two mynas, and three bird cages. Cicil was sure that no life was spared in the attack, as she had closely watched the scene through her specam.

"Were there only 18 people in those two speed boats? Did the assailants take away some of the passengers?" I wanted to ask these things to Cicil, but I was in a terrible shock. I had never seen such a horrific scene in my life. Though Cicil was also shaken by the incident, she whispered into my ears, "They took away 11 people, including men and women; they also looted the belongings of the passengers."

In the meantime, Vasan commanded, "Switch off the headlights, boats are coming this way from the South."

Those boats were not coming to the area where we were, but travelling in a direction far away from us. We could spot five headlights. In minutes, fireworks lit up the sky, followed by gun shots.

"They are Sea Tigers. They will not allow anyone to outsmart them, especially the people of their own community," said Vasan as though to himself.

By the light of the fireworks, we could see five boats surrounded by three vessels.

Cicil wanted our boat to be taken to that spot. But Vasan discouraged her. We heard sporadic guns shots, and it lasted for an hour.

Watching everything through her specam, she told us, "All the people onboard the boat have been taken captive and shifted to a dhow and they are returning. I can also make out a few people out there. Let's go."

Vasan did not object to it. Switching off the headlight, we took our boat to that spot. On reaching, we switched on the lights and what we saw was heart-breaking. It was like a battle field; we found dead bodies of three old men and five elderly women, and some broken household items floating scattered in the sea. Three among the victims were seen wearing thick sacks over their dresses which they might had put on to protect themselves from sea wind. We also found three cats and four dogs with their bellies filled with sea water. The same night, fourteen more boats sped away from the South to North. The Sri Lankan Navy destroyed four of them and the Sea Tigers captured seven. Only three boats could break through the defence lines and survive.

A seemingly fed up Vasan said, "Dawn is about to break; I think there won't be any more encounters with other vessels."

Cicil countered Vasan and asked him," Encounter! We were witnessing a battle to 'conquer or surrender'."

In a fit of anger, she added, "This is fleeing; a desperate run to escape death. Here, a word like encounter holds no meaning!"

To borrow Cicil's words, the aluminum vessels and plastic buckets floating in the sea were the balance sheets of each of the conquests. There could be seven, eight or even ten corpses along with them. And also, those of animals and birds which were pampered by their masters when they were alive. They had left this world along with their loving masters.

"Our mission is over. What is next? Let us go back..."

Vasan's dispassionate words annoyed Cicil. She told me, "I want to watch the sea in the daylight. Our story must go on air in the backdrop of this horrific aftermath of a battle."

Vasan was confused. Noticing that, I told him, "She is right. We must reach there."

He agreed. "Let us go. We will take the boat to the islet. I have enough food for you guys not just for today, but for the entire week; it is stored in the escort boat."

It was a horrible day. The sea did not leave any signs of cruelties we witnessed the previous night. An eerie peace prevailed and we could not even find a piece of cloth, let alone dead bodies, even after searching for hours. Calm seas, transparent water. Where has the sea, that erases everything, hidden the last night?

We wandered in the sea for quite some time. Sathyamma was sitting crouched in a corner of the boat in utter silence. Immersed in our search, we had almost forgotten her. Cicil, who was about to speak something on our next move, accidentally locked her eyes with Sathyamma's. In a tone suffused with an emotion which cannot be described as guilt or repentance or compassion, she muttered, "What can we do for this woman...?"

Before she completed it, Sathyamma said, "My children didn't die in the sea. Had they been killed, their bodies would have floated towards me. Because, I love them so much."

After a pause, she continued.

"The sea does not keep the dead bodies in her custody. She sends them where they deserve to be."

After keeping quiet for a while, she requested us,

"My children could not have died... Nobody can think of killing such beautiful young girls. They might have been sexually exploited and dumped somewhere on the Lankan shore. Please be kind enough to drop me on the Sri Lankan shore."

An empathetic Cicil seemed to have decided on something. She did not even consult me on that. She moved closer to Sathyamma and asked her. "Can you wait for one more night? We have a little more work to do here."

"I will wait to see my daughters."

Cicil was preparing herself for a daring mission to reveal something the world was not aware of, on the brutalities that led to the mass exodus from the war-stricken Sri Lanka to India. "Until then I will have no rest. I want to show the unseen face of war to the world."

She discussed her plan with me in detail: "How many people are being killed in attacks and accidents while they flee Lanka? How many have disappeared in the sea? How many have been kidnapped? Let us show the world the faceless victims of war, including the ones we witnessed being killed today."

I agreed to her idea. When I told her how connected were Sathyamma and my families, her interest in the woman grew, and she promised to find her kidnapped daughters at any cost.

I encouraged her. In between, I told her about Sathayamma and the family connections we shared. On hearing that she was the daughter of a noble soul and a personification of Love called Poilapillai, Cicil showed more affection and respect towards Sathyamma. She was now determined to locate her children at any cost; she told me that would suit our professional interests too.

We were waiting for an eventful night. It will take one more hour for our boats to come.

I looked at my watch. It is 11.54 P.M.

April 22, 2008

Tuesday

We had anchored our boat in the sea. It was an unusually dark night and at half past one, we spotted the headlight of a speed boat. When it sped past us to the North, Cicil was worried, "Have they changed their base?"

Vasan, who knew the sea route better than anyone present there, said:

"Whether it is the Tigers or the Sri Lankan Navy, they can block the boats only along this stretch, as there are many sand beds and sea rocks under the water. To reach the Indian shore, this stretch is the safest route. In other areas, an experienced boat driver can escape the eyes of the gunmen, but they cannot do it here because if they try any tricks, their boats will hit the rocks or the sand beds, and the boats will capsize."

In the meantime, two more boats went past us. Within an hour, far away in the South and out of our eyesight, a few gunshots rang out; in a few minutes, something went up in flames.

Vasan said, "It seems a diesel tank has been hit."

Whatever it may be, by the time we reached there, the boat and the its passengers would be burnt to ashes. Even then, we would have gone there, but a strong wind and huge waves stalled our progress. Though Vasan said it was better to anchor the boat close to the shore, Cicil was adamant that we should press ahead.

It took almost an hour for us to reach there. Adding to our difficulties, it rained heavily and the debris of the boat and charred bodies floated in the sea. When we reached there braving heavy odds, we experienced for ourselves the fury of rain gods in the sea. Cicil was busy capturing the scene in her specam. We heard a loud cry and Vasan focussed the headlight to that direction. He said, "It seems a boat has capsized."

Ignoring the howling wind and furious rains, we tried to reach the spot. We saw there a drowning boat and some hands desperately calling out for our help. But, we could not help anyone. Cicil, after counting thirteen dead bodies, said with a heavy heart,

"Who knows the people who die like this? Who can provide their names and other details? The Sri Lankan government or the Indian government? Are these people not human beings?"

The fact that we could not save a single person made us feel guilty feeling and terribly exhausted.

Our boat was being tossed by the sea waves under heavy rain. While Cicil was explaining to me the scenes she had recorded in her specam, I noticed that she was sleepy. In fact, I was also feeling sleepy. It didn't take too long for both of us to slip into a sleep.

Vasan woke us up, "Aren't you feeling hungry? Get up please?" Then only we knew it was already noon.

The sky looked cloudy and dark, and may be because of the cool sea breeze and exhaustion we had overslept.

It was only after having the lunch that we realised the capability and care of Vasan which boosted our confidence in him to a great extent. We told him that and appreciated his invaluable services to our mission.

Then, Vasan threw at us a big question. "Isn't the work in the sea over? What is next?"

Cicil replied immediately.

"We want to go to the very starting point of the exodus. To that spot from where Sathyammas begin their flight, surely with the help of this Sathyamma...

You should take us to the Lankan shore at the very earliest, and of course, all other help that we may require there."

Vasan smiled.

"Madam, no problem at all. Not just to the shore, I know very well that you may even venture out into the deep interiors of Sri Lanka. Please remember, this is an act of infiltration to a foreign land without a visa. But, don't worry, I will ensure that you will not face any problems there. Today, surveillance by the coast guard is very strong and hence you can reach the Lankan shore only after eleven in the night."

Vasan continued, "In half an hour's time my partner who is the in-charge of our operations at the sea will come to receive you. He will take you for sightseeing in the sea until eleven, thereafter he will entrust you to the care of my Lankan counterpart. Don't think that they are like me, but I myself. May be, they are known to you and know you very well."

As told by Vasan, in half-an-hour, a luxury boat arrived near us. From its deck, a handsome young man welcomed us.

"I am Twan Rabeer. Welcome on board…"

When we entered in the boat, he slowly whispered into my ear.

"Have you forgotten me?"

"No. I haven't."

It was the same jovial fellow who took me all around the Andaman Islands for about five days at one stage of Vasantha case. I haven't seen anyone who was so much in love with seas or as knowledgeable of the sea as him.

After giving us Sathyamma and our luggage, Vasan bade good bye to us and said, "Come back victorious! I will be here to pick you."

The boat was entirely different from the previous ones, and it had all the comforts and luxuries of a five-star hotel.

Rabeer's jokes and pleasant conversation kept us happy throughout the journey. After a sumptuous dinner, our vessel docked at a private wharf on the Lankan shore at eleven. Rabeer did not come out of the boat. A dark, stout man came to receive us, to whom he said,

"These guys are Vasan's priceless guests. Protect them like divine gifts."

Then, he turned to me and said, "Entire Sri Lanka is under his control. Accomplish your mission and come back. I will be here to receive you."

It was Dhammika Pereira, the Sri Lankan counterpart of Vasan. He looked at me and guffawed. He had travelled with me to the interiors of Sri Lanka on several occasions. Therefore, he knew me and my missions very well.

He took us to his own guest house near the wharf. Dhammika also stayed there.

"Now, have some sleep. We will chart tomorrow's programme in the morning."

Cicil, not willing to leave Sathyamma alone, took her to her room.

I was about to sleep in a foreign country without permission.

I looked at my watch. It is 11.55 P.M.

April 23, 2008

Wednesday

We woke up into a day full of surprises. There was a packet on the table along with the daily newspapers. On opening it, we were stunned to see all the necessary documents needed for our hassle-free travel across Sri Lanka.

They included an entry pass, a travel-sheet that would permit us to visit any part of the country and press cards for us as media persons- all of them had our photographs and necessary signatures and official stamps! Dhammika had arranged everything for us, who had entered the country illegally without passports and visas, without even submitting applications.

The next surprise was at the dining table. We found a file on the table, containing complete details of

Sathyamma. With great curiosity, we leafed through it. The only information which we found new was that Sathayamma and her family's decision to escape to India was taken all of a sudden, and not a pre-planned one. She was living in a place called Vaka near Jaffna. She sold her house and the land at a throwaway price and fled to India with her family by paying that money as ferry charges.

Her property was bought by a middleman named Kumaran, a tobacco dealer. He later demolished that house and built a makeshift go-down for his business.

Cicil failed to find words to appreciate Dhammika enough for his good work. He arranged all those documents within a single day.

Praising him to the skies, she asked Dhammika, "Who are you exactly, dear Dhammika? What an amazing network you are having! Where did you get our photographs from?"

Dhammika replied with a humble smile. "Madam, I am your host here. My mission is to understand your needs and provide you support to the best of my ability. If my work has made you happy, I am overwhelmed. Arranging this lady's details and your travel documents were a cake-walk for me. As for these photographs, they are readily available on the net." With amazing self-confidence, he continued, "When I am with you, these documents are not required at all. But I arranged them just to make you comfortable and tension-free."

By then the real problem arose before us; it was Dhammika who brought it to our attention.

"You want to know from where Sathyamma began her journey, am I right? When her house does not exist any longer, what is the point in going there now?"

"We will go there, anyway," Cicil said firmly. "Only her house is not there. That's only a lifeless thing. But the place where she was born, where she lived and the things that made her are very much there..."

When Cicil said this, Sathyamma began to weep. She was listening to our conversations intently.

Ccsil continued, saying she had made an error.

"The house is not the issue. Our prime concern is to locate her children, for which we need to go there." To lighten the tense atmosphere, she smiled and said, "There is an adage in the Norwegian language: When a person goes missing, the search should not start from that very spot where he was last seen, but at his home and nearby places."

Dhammika nodded in agreement.

Then there was no delay. Dhammika joined us with some of his aides.

Gloom filled the air. We travelled with a feeling that yet another catastrophe was lying in wait for us. Throughout our journey, we could see the scars of war. Collapsed buildings, closed schools, destroyed bridges and so on.

We found dark-skinned, unsmiling people everywhere. Children were skinny and malnourished. Insecurity reflected in every movement they made. Women, with despair written large on their faces, peered at us from the front of rare open shops. But the faces of security personnel deployed along the roads at regular intervals to inspect people and vehicles had cruelty written all over them.

However, it seemed all of them were afraid of Dhammika. Could it be respect? Who knows? At every halting point, when he raised his hands, our vehicle was allowed to go through sans customary inspection and security checks.

Again, same scenes, closed schools and damaged buildings.

Cicil asked, "Is this the school vacation time or what?"

Dhammika replied, "Schools here have been shut for ages."

"Why?" She asked again.

Dhammika's answered diplomatically.

"Apart from the external factors you guys use normally describe like conflicts, war or encounters, there is another aspect; most parents refuse to send their children to the schools."

Dhammika stopped for a while and continued.

"Tigers want kids to join their juvenile army. They will get them in batches from schools. Children are used to collect information from houses. Here, almost all the houses have links to the Tigers. Police and military kidnap kids from schools and use them to ferret out such secrets. Kidnapping children from schools is easy for them."

Dhammika took a deep breath and said: "What a misfortune! A generation is denied even education."

An indignant Cicil was about to say something when the sight of a mother and child caught our attention. She was carrying an infant in her arms, and was mercilessly beating up a boy who was following her. The seven-year-old was crying without any protest, and she kept on beating him. When he fell down, she began kicking the child, to our horror.

"Stop it," Cicil shouted as soon as our vehicle reached near them. When it stopped, we saw at close quarters the fury of the mother and the utter helplessness of her son. "Ask the woman why is she assaulting the boy..." She asked Dhammika.

The woman tried to run away just as we stopped the vehicle. Dhammika stopped her, saying, "We are not Tigers or police. Why are you beating up the child?"

In between sobs, she told Dhammika what had happened. Dhammika kept looking at the ground as she spoke and later, he narrated to us her plight.

She lived three kilometers away, and came there to buy rice and kerosene for which she sold off some of her personal belongings. Shops remained close in her locality; even if they opened, essential commodities were not available. She had purchased one kilogramme of rice and one litre of kerosene after a long wait of three hours in the queue.

The price for one kilogramme of rice was Rupees 290, and one litre of kerosene cost Rupees 410. That is, Rs 700 was shelled out to buy them!

She was tired carrying her infant in one of her arms and that was why she had given the rice bag and kerosene bottle, which she was holding in her other hand, to her son. But the bag and kerosene bottle slipped out of his hands, the bottle was broken and the precious rice got drenched in kerosene.

She was telling Dhammika, "Now tell me sir, how can I forgive him?"

Prices of the essential commodities surprised me. I saw Cicil taking out her wallet.

I asked Dhammika. "Rice and kerosene cost this high?"

He said, "It is cheaper here. In certain areas, one kilogramme of rice costs Rupees 350, and one litre kerosene Rupees 700."

Cicil extended a few currency notes to that woman, and told us like a teacher. "The inevitable by-product of a civil war is scarcity. Whether it is in Africa or in the erstwhile Soviet Union, the clouds of civil unrest will always rain down scarcities. This is a universal truth. Scarcity will create steep price rise. Value of currencies will fall and there have been instances when they came to naught..."

However, the woman refused to accept the money. She asked Dhammika to tell her to accept the money and buy the commodities she had lost.

Dhammika did not answer. Instead, he gave an indication to the driver, who in turn went to the accompanying vehicle and took from it one can of kerosene and a four kg rice bag and gave them to the woman.

As if chanced upon a treasure, her sunken eyes brightened. Her lips shivered with unspoken words of gratitude and tears trickled down her eyes.

Cicil was happy and she kept looking at the woman. They talked to each other in a language without words and sounds. The woman was smiling very happily.

"This is Punya. This is divine." Sathyamma, who had been quiet till then, said.

Cicil turned to me and said, “I am seeing a smiling Sathyamma for the first time, after we touched the Lankan soil.”

While the woman put her child down and sat on the floor holding the rice bag close to her chest, Dhammika said, “Let’s go.”

When the vehicle started moving, Cicil asked Dhammika. “Let me repeat the question I asked you in the morning. Who are you really? I saw you helping people without being asked. Could you please reveal yourself?”

Dhammika smiled, and said. “I know we are going to a place where everything is scarce. So, I have taken enough precautions. I just gave her a little from that.”

He continued to narrate the situation prevailing there, and on why people continued to flee the area. Most of them were what Vasan had already told us.

Our vehicle stopped in front of a godown in a desolate property. A dark, lean man who looked like an ordinary worker came out. The driver told him something in private, and he ran outside.

Sathyamma got out of the vehicle weeping.

"This is the place where my house stood, Oh God, everything has been wiped out."

She looked all around and cried again.

"The land where my children used to play..."

She squatted on the ground, placed her hands on the earth and said, "This soil was so dear to my husband. I left it without realising its true value."

She sank to her knees and touched her face to the soil abruptly. She stayed in that posture for quite some time. When I helped her to her feet, she told me very privately. "I heard the soil speaking to me. It asked me why did I leave her and cursed me. It kept on asking me about my children, taking the names of each of them. It is asking me, where are her friends..."

A man came along with the worker who had earlier gone outside. He shivered at the sight of Dhammika.

"Had I known you were interested in this property, I would not have purchased it." He stopped for a while and said in a tone of complete surrender.

"It is now all yours. Take it please."

Dhammika smiled. Then he patted the shoulder of the man and asked.

"What is your name?"

He said, "Kumaran."

"Kumaran, I am not that Dhammika whom you have heard of. If I need any land, I will tell you, and I will pay for it. Now, I am looking for this lady's children."

It was then that Kumaran saw Sathyamma.

In a voice still gripped by fear, he asked Sathyamma, "Sathyamma, where is Savithri? Where are Saroja and Sathyavathi? Our Sivarathnam?"

I intervened and asked: "Who is Sivarathnam?"

"Her son," Kumaran said. "She left for India with all her four children. She sold her property to me for paying the boat charges."

I intervened again. "She is not speaking anything about her son. She is very particular that we don't ask anything about him."

Kumaran looked at Sathyamma, took us aside and said: "Sivarathnam is a smart boy. After his father's death, Sathyamma earned money by offering tuitions. But it was Sivarathnam who looked after the entire family. He could do any kind of work. He was in love with a Sinhalese girl, Dilini and that was the only flaw he had.

As it was an alliance not suitable for Tamil community, Sathyamma opposed it, but her sisters liked the girl. I know only this much about him," added Kumaran.

Then I realised why Sathyamma barred me from asking about her son. I got it!

Dhammika asked.

"What is our plan? Should we meet Dilini and ask her about the whereabouts of Sivarathnam, or enquire about the daughters of Sathyamma?"

Cicil asserted, "We have to do both."

When Sathyamma got into the vehicle, Dhammika gave some instructions to his aides. When he returned to Kumaran to bid good bye, he bowed to Dhammika and said, "I have something to tell you in private."

Then he took us a little farther and said in hushed tones, "Those girls had some links with the Tigers. Sathyamma left for India taking all of them so that her daughters would be forced to cut off their Tiger-connections. By revealing all these things, I exposed myself to danger. My life is in your hands."

"You need not worry. You will be safe." Giving him that assurance, Dhammika got into the vehicle.

Sathyamma was extremely tired. But without

consulting us, Dhammika asked her.

"Did your daughters have any connections with the Tigers? If they had, why didn't you tell us?"

Though she was very weak, her reply was boomed.

"I am their mother. I need my daughters."

Not only Dhammika, we too did not ask her anything further. But, she kept on repeating those words.

During our journey, Dhammika's satellite phone and walkie-talkie kept on chattering. A vehicle following us overtook us and entered a narrow lane. Our vehicle followed it.

After a short drive, our vehicle stopped before a middle-class house, built in old Sinhalese style.

One man from the vehicle that overtook us entered the house. Soon, he returned with a middle-aged man, who looked like the man of the house. They took us in; Sathyamma got down from the vehicle and came along with us very reluctantly.

The house owner was in some sense of panic. However, he introduced himself to us and told Dhammika. "I know you. I am Fernando, Dilini's father. I was told you wanted to ask her something. You may ask her whatever you want. She is here." He glanced at Sathyamma, and said, "I have no objection to give away my daughter in marriage to her son."

Then he called his daughter. Dark in complexion, Dilini looked smart and beautiful. She was a teacher with an international school. As the school was closed for vacation, she was back at her home. She did not forget to greet Sathyamma.

Dilini answered all the cunning questions from Cicil with full confidence. She understood the purpose of our visit and did not hide anything. She told us everything she knew.

Sivaratham and she were in love; if she was to marry anyone, he would surely be her lover, though his mother and sisters had different opinions. Sivarathnam told her that he would come back after taking his mother and sisters to India. So, she was waiting for him. This was what Dilini had to say.

That was the continuation of some important piece of information. Dhammika doubted whether there was more information on the LTTE links of which Kumaran hinted at. All of a sudden, he said:

"We have been able to gather some clues on

Sivarathnam and his sisters. We want to find and hand over them to their mother, for which Dilini must support us. Tell us what all you know. Don't be afraid."

When Dilini hesitated, Dhammika continued, "We know very well that those girls had joined the Tigers. We also understand whether Sivarathnam, though a sympathiser of Tigers, wanted to save his sisters from the terror outfit. Now, all the four are missing. Have you something more to add, Dilini?"

His question really surprised us, which showed the kind of experience and intelligence he had. We even wondered whether it was this natural ability that helped him to have people with intelligence, education, physical prowess and practical knowledge at his beck and call. Even as my thoughts wandered, Dilini opened up.

Her father encouraged her and told her, "Tell them dear girl, whatever you know. It is an attempt to find your beloved Rathnam and his sisters."

Dilini continued. "Yes, Sivarathnam was an LTTE supporter. At the same time, he did not want his sisters to be part of the group. Sivarathnam strongly opposed it when Tigers tried to force his sisters into becoming human bombs. But the sisters, brainwashed by Tigers, rejected his warnings.

"Once he told me that since his sisters were under suggestion, they didn't have the discretionary powers to understand the truth and withdraw from LTTE. Rathnam revealed to me that Mediforce of the Tigers had developed techniques to make a person do whatever it commanded by the use of psychiatric medicines, including drugs and psychological methods like hypnosis. He was worried that his sisters were being trained for an unknown mission.

"Once, when Sivarathnam challenged their strategy, the deputy commander told him, 'We have dedicated ourselves to a great aim. Relationships are immaterial to us. The only important thing is the successful completion of our mission.' For Rathnam, that argument was unacceptable. But, Rathnam resisted again. Then the commander warned him, 'You think we are going to kill your mother and sisters or even you to solve this problem? You are mistaken. We will pierce your beloved Dilini's beautiful eyes. Then chop each of her organs: her breasts, her ears, and if you still don't agree with us, you will witness how my Tiger cubs tear her apart. Beware!'

"Completely shaken by the threat, he wandered like

a mad man. During those days, he had a chance meeting with Athiran, an agent who ferried people to India. Athiran assured him that he will take his mother and sisters to India at Rs13,000 per head. His mother agreed and as soon as she heard it, sold their house and left the same day after giving the money to Athiran.

Rathnam had met me before their journey began from Yazhini, under the cover of night. He had assured me that he would come back. I told him I don't mind if Tigers pierced my eyes and took away my organs, but I won't be reborn if I was thrown to the Tiger cubs.

"He walked away with his head bowed. That was the last time I saw him. I looked on until my eyes could follow him."

After this detailed explanation, she consoled us. "I am sure he will come back. Nothing will happen to him. You know, we have to live together. Whatever may happen, he will come back. He will."

She repeated it as if she felt that we did not take her words seriously.

"We have decided on everything. We know, after betraying the Tigers we cannot have a peaceful life here. So, we have decided to move to Kandy and settle there.

There, nobody will suspect a Buddhist couple leading a pious life. Or else, we will go to Rameshwaram."

We doubted whether this girl was losing her mental balance. Cicil also had the same feeling. She threw me a meaningful glance.

Dhammika intervened and said affectionately.

"That's okay. We got the information we wanted".

While we were leaving, her father came to our vehicle. He complained, "We face threats from both sides. Woman Tigers threaten my daughter seeking information on Sivarathnam and his sisters. For the same information, the police and the military are also troubling us. Sir, please save us from this dilemma."

As our vehicle began moving, Dhammika said. "The matter is serious when both the Tigers and the Police are after you!"

Then he looked at Sathyamma, and asked, "Do you know anything?"

Sathyamma's reply was a loud wail.

"I want my children..."

Cicil asked Dhammika not to ask her any questions

from then on.

Dhammika began talking to someone on his walkie-talkie and also on the phone. He gave some directions to the driver; it seemed he got the reply he wanted.

"We are now going to meet the Deputy Chief of Military Intelligence. If the Government has any information on them, we will get it now," he said.

I think we travelled for almost an hour-and-a-half. Before we reached the gate of the Intelligence Regional Office of the Military, Dhammika took us inside the highly secured fort-like building with such assurance that it seemed he was taking us to his own house.

The Deputy Chief was waiting for us in his chamber.

"I am Chamath Abhayasinge," he introduced himself.

Then he explained to us, "Those for whom Dhammika is on the lookout are neither in our custody nor with the police or in jails. The reason why I asked you to come here is that none of those who have been caught are known by their own names. Most of them have fake names. I will show you some photographs. Please see whether you can find the persons you are looking for..."

Cicil looked at Sathyamma. She looked calm.

We were shocked to see some of the photographs that Chamath spread out on the table. Most of them were heads without bodies, that too with disfigured faces and bearing bullet marks. Sathaymma, who looked at those photographs with great curiosity, uttered only one word at last. 'NO'.

Chamath looked at us for a moment and told Dhammika.

"Now there are only two possibilities. Either they may have been killed in the sea or could be at one of the Tiger camps."

It seemed he was not bothered about the fact that he was saying this in front of a mother.

When we got out of his cabin, he called us again into his cabin leaving Sathyamma outside and said in a low voice.

"Forgive me. So far, I was delivering the official version for you. In fact, all those four were under our surveillance. We had even been tipped off that they were being readied for a special mission. But somehow they escaped from us at the last minute."

He clasped the hands of Dhammika and said.

"Brother, one more thing. We have unconfirmed reports that some of them have taken asylum at the Holy Home. As you know, we cannot enter the place."

"Let me see," Dhammika said firmly. While we were leaving the place, Cicil whispered into my ear, "Nice shots. I have recorded the pictures of all those severed heads in my specam."

Even before we left the gates of Intelligence Headquarters, Dhammika was firing some instructions to someone on his satellite phone.

"Pick up Athiran."

Then, turning to us, he said, "Let us go to Holy Home."

We had no idea what Holy Home was.

Dhammika explained to us all about the institution.

Jeevantha Jayakkodi, a Buddhist rebel and highly respected figure all over Sri Lanka, runs the Holy Home, a shelter for the destitute. He did not discriminate between homeless people on the basis of their religion, language, ethnic identity etc. and welcomed all to his Holy Home. A true saint. He was equally unacceptable to religious organisations, the Srilankan government and Tigers. But, he was hugely popular due to his noble deeds. It is heard that the majority of the inmates in the Holy Home were psychologically challenged women.

Immediately, after giving us this brief introduction, Dhammika said in a low voice, "I may not be acceptable there. Nevertheless, we must have to go there as part of our mission. We should not miss a single chance to accomplish our objective."

Cicil asked, "You are acceptable and welcome everywhere. Then what is the problem here?"

Dhammika's reply came pat.

"He is a fearless man as he has nothing to gain or lose."

His response contained all the answers. We didn't ask anything further.

What awaited at the Holy Home was something very shocking. As we got down from the vehicle after it entered home, a stark naked woman came running and stood before us, with untied hair and exposed breasts; she suddenly lay before us with a weird expression and spread her legs. "You people share my body between you and have your fill... But please leave my child alone. She is just a little kid..."

We were taken aback, not knowing what to do and could not say anything, and she kept repeating the same words.

It was then that I noticed, her eyes were shut tight!

Suddenly some women came running and got her to her feet; with great kindness, they took her inside.

On learning that he had guests, an old man came out. Dhammika told us in a whisper, "Jeevantha".

He greeted us: "Whoever you may be, I welcome all of you like Gods… Though there may even be devils among gods at times."

Dhammika was distinctly uncomfortable. Without paying any attention to Dhammika's discomfort, he took us to the reception room.

"I know Dhammika. But I don't know any of you. What can I do for you?"

After introducing ourselves, I told him about the purpose of our visit.

"Nobody lives here by those names. Most of the

inmates here are like the people whom you saw just now – those who are emotionally unstable."

After slipping into silence for a while, he said, "Perhaps their real names are different from those I know. So please meet the inmates here in person... May be, those you are looking for among them."

He walked inside, we followed him.

In the limited amenities of the home, there lived a large joint family of mothers, children, young girls and elderly women. Sathyamma carefully looked at the faces of each of them. We saw disappointment on her face while withdrawing her gaze from each inmate.

Jeevantha called each one of the inmates by name and introduced them to us. Among them were mentally, physically and visually challenged persons. Sathyamma was searching for her daughters in each of them.

Without naming her, he gestured to a woman to come near. We were surprised to see it was the same woman who shocked us with her nudity. She was properly dressed and behaved decently.

"She is Rani," Jeevantha said.

Cicil exclaimed, "This is incredible! Why did she behave in that manner then?"

Jeevantha asked her to go and then told us her story. She was living at Palali near Jaffna with her parents, husband and an 11-year-old daughter. Their lives turned topsy-turvy when Tigers compelled them to join LTTE, while the police frequented their house to find out whether they had any Tiger connections. Caught between them, misfortune became their regular visitor. Her aged parents were killed and her husband was kidnapped and murdered. Who were the people behind her husband's murder, she did not know; but his body was found a week later on a road side, with his tongue cut. Thereafter, her life became too miserable to live and she realised that the life of her daughter was not safe.

So, she decided to escape to her parental country–India.

She knew that she had to have lots of money to pay the agents who smuggled people to India. She would have to pay Rs14,000 to the boat agent. The only way she could find that much money in those troubled times was to sell herself. She took weekly trips to Sea View in Jaffna for fourteen weeks and earned Rs14,000, at Rs1,000 a day. I would have hated her had she gone there for a fifteenth time. An unconscious mind cannot lie and it was her unconscious mind that told me, she went there fourteen times. It was money thus earned that was used for her ill-fated boat journey to India.

Jeevantha continued, "However, her boat was attacked in the middle of the sea. She did not know who the attackers were, but she was brutally gang-raped by them. They did not even spare her 11-year-old daughter. When the cries of her daughter rent the air, she threw away the clothes she wore, stood naked before them and offered herself so that her child would be spared. But she had to remain a mute spectator when her child, drenched in blood, was raped again and again after which they threw away her lifeless body into the sea, like a rag-doll.

"She was brought here by Ahammad Ali, a Malayalee man who runs a hotel named Malabar Café. He took a lot of trouble to bring her, who was lying unconscious on the sea shore, to this home. It has been almost six months since she came here and she strips down whenever she sees strangers. It is said that there are no wounds that Time cannot heal, but I wonder whether Time can heal the wounds of a mother like her."

Cicil couldn't control herself and sobbed. Sathyamma, standing a little away in a state of numbness, was looking for someone.

Jeevantha said, addressed to none in particular: "She is just one among a thousand such cases."

He called another girl, and introduced her again. "Look at this girl. She is Sasika. After killing everyone in her family and her relatives, the assailants cut off her breasts. I am sure even Shurpanakha did not have to go through such an ordeal. She became mentally derailed and took to wandering the streets aimlessly. She was brought here by Anusha Bhandaraka, a social worker."

He paused for a moment, and raised his hands in the sky and muttered as though to himself, "You know, half of the children here are mentally challenged. How can one not lose his/her mind when dear-ones are brutally killed right before their eyes with bombs and guns?"

Cicil sobbed like a child, and sat down on the floor. I doubted whether Sathyamma was hearing all these. She stood motionless like a statue.

Jeevantha helped Cicil to get up and like a father, he consoled her. "My child, come with me. Let's have some rest tonight."

While taking us inside the home, he was heard speaking to himself. "The wounds a war leave behind are beyond our comprehension. Those wounds will never heal, even after the war is over."

On the way to the guest room, he stared at Dhammika. I felt there was a curse burning in that pointed glare. While serving food to us, he said," I am looking for the rights among a heap of wrongs. The discrimination being practised by the Sinhalese is wrong; the Tamils' fight for separate homeland is also wrong. They shouldn't go for a vivisection of the country in the name of Tamil identity. Killing as well as getting killed are equally unjustifiable. Who are the wrongdoers? Who can correct themselves?"

"Snatching lives of others knowing very well that one cannot give it back, isn't that wrong? Isn't denying children love and care, depriving them of basic human rights like education wrong? Can anybody give me single right reason to believe they are not wrong? I am trying to find one right thing among this mountain of wrongs!"

Stopping his introspection abruptly, he said, "It seems I've bored all of you. I can distinguish between human beings and devils. I was talking to myself, or rather to the human beings."

Dhammika got the connotations in Jeevantha's charged words.

Realising that, Jeevanthika continued, "Dhammika can put this Holy Home to flames in a minute if he really wishes so. Nobody will question him. Mr Dhammika, you can expand your empire by keeping your feet in both boats. You are an adviser and aide to both the government and the Tigers simultaneously. Remember, if the country is not there, you also cease to exist. Set free this country from your clutches of greed."

We were shell-shocked to see his frontal, brutal assault on Dhammika, a man who can move mountains. But he did not protest and it seemed he was enjoying the impassioned speech of Jeevantha.

Suddenly Jeevantha turned towards us.

"You have come here after a long journey. You can have your rest here tonight and leave tomorrow early morning. Dhammika is here; if he wants, he can take you even to the dens of the Tigers, and look for your children."

We felt that statement also didn't make an impact on Dhammika.

When Jeevantha left the room, Dhammika told us.

"All those outbursts were directed at me. Still I have high regards for him. I have never seen such a fearless person in all my life."

I also wrote in my diary, I too haven't seen a person like him.

Now, the time is 11.57 P.M.

April 24, 2008

Thursday

"Get up. We have to go now". Dhammika's excited call woke me up.

When I looked at my watch it was three in the morning.

I could not understand what he was saying as I was half asleep. He returned with Sathyamma and Cicil and repeated, "Get a move on, guys. We have nabbed Athiran, the boatman who helped Sathyamma and her daughters escape to India. My boys managed to get hold of him and he is in their custody."

Sleep evaporated instantly, and I saw Sathyamma and Cicil all set for the journey.

Jeeyantha Jayakkodi, who was wide wake, approached us. In an empathetic tone he said," Perhaps, you will get crucial information that will lead you to the missing girls. May God bless you in your mission. Start immediately. If you find the children to be burdensome, send them to me. I will take good care of them."

Dhammika directed the driver, "Check point at Kem Nine."

The road was desolate, but tough to navigate. However, at certain points, some people came to inspect our vehicles, but on seeing Dhammika they withdrew. It took us almost one-and-a-half hour to hit the main road.

The check point at Kem Nine was a peculiar one. The first check point was on the side of Sri Lanka, where the inspecting personnel were in military uniform. After that, it was the Tiger's check point. In between there was a no man's land where nobody was in control. Vehicles were permitted to move only after the inspections by both the Tigers and Sri Lankan military.

But our vehicle was not inspected either by the Sri Lankan force or the Tigers.

After being greeted by both sides, our vehicles turned left from the main road and moved a little further before stopping. There, two trucks stood side by side in opposite directions, with some space in between. Someone directed a spotlight to the place in between the trucks and the sight frightened us out of our wits. There was a man hanging in the air; his one each of his hands and legs were tied to the back of one truck and his other limbs were tied to the other truck. It looked as if he was lying on his back, in the air!

Dhammika slowly moved into the light. He was not the Dhammika we saw at the home of Jeevantha. Only words that reeked of death and destruction escaped his mouth.

"These trucks will move in opposite directions in two minutes and you will be torn into two then. If you have anything to say, make it fast. I want to know what happened to Sivarathnam and his sisters."

Without any signs of protest, the man said, "It was a fake boat mishap enacted in the middle of the sea as per the directions of Sivarathnam. He himself handed over his sisters to Tamil Tigers amid the turmoil, and dragged his mother to another boat in the guise of saving her from attackers."

"Sivarathnam did this to rescue his girlfriend Dilina. The Tigers demanded the custody of his sisters who were being trained to become suicide bombers. They threatened him that if he did not return his sisters in 24 hours, his girlfriend would be gangraped, mutilated and subjected to unspeakable cruelties.

"Dilini had already informed Sivarathnam of the threat to her life, and he was well aware of the situation."

Athiran admitted it was he who acted as a messenger between the two sides.

At the end of confessions, he convulsed in pain and pleaded for water. But Dhammika didn't seem to care and his tone toughened. Actually, it was much more than third degree torture.

"To whom did he exchange the girls? Who took them away? When?"

Athiran replied:" The girls were handed over to Dr Kathirvel. His men arrived at the beach in a vehicle to take them away."

"Where is Sivarathnam?"

"He escaped to India in some other boat."

"What is his plan?"

"After securing a job, take Dilini with him and settle there forever."

"Do you know where he is now?"

"I don't know. He cannot go anywhere leaving the shore and the sea."

"Where were the girls taken to?"

"I don't know."

Athiran asked for water again and wriggled in the air in acute pain.

Dhammika ordered his aide to put out the light and took us to our vehicle. After ensuring that we all got into the vehicle, he looked back and shouted.

"Start the vehicle and push off."

As we were leaving, we heard the sound of moving trucks and the crackle of breaking bones, accompanied by a frightening scream.

Cicil got scared and whispered to me, "Heart-numbing!"

Then she asked Dhammika, "Was it necessary?"

He replied, "Very much. There was no other way to make him reveal the truth. If I spare his life, Tigers will come to know about this, and it will strain our relations."

We could see a suppressed smile on his face when he

said, "Whoever happens to see his body will easily understand who did this."

An eerie silence filled the vehicle. Nobody talked for a while.

Cicil's excited whisper reached my ears. "I have everything in my specam, except Athiran's brutal end."

Dhammika might have felt that we were blaming him. He told us, "Whatever I am doing is for you alone. I am duty-bound to assist you in this mission and to protect your interests."

But, we did not say anything. Then, he surprised us with an announcement.

"We are now heading straight to the Tigers' den."

Our excitement knew no bounds, and Cicil had always dreamt of shooting at such a place. I asked him, "Is it possible to enter a Tigers' den?"

Before I got an answer, Cicil threw another, with child-like curiosity.

"Would it be possible for us to meet Prabhakaran?"

Interrupting us, Sathyamma began weeping, "My dear children..."

Dhammika told us, "Let us fulfill our duty first. Our first task is to meet Dr Kathirvel, who took custody of the girls. I think Professor Vaidyalingam, an advisor and guru of Tigers, can take us to Dr Kathirvel. Vaidyalingam would be around and help us reach the Tigers' den."

Even now, Cicil was anxious whether we could meet Prabhakaran or not.

Dhammika did not answer.

"I heard that he is a coward who never shows up before the world. Is that true?"

Dhammika did not like the question and reacted rather sharply.

"What did you think of Prabhakaran? A coward? I know him very well. We studied together in school. He was brave and fearless even in those days. He is capable of doing anything and everything. You know, his dangerous journey in revolution started with a single match stick. In the year 1974, when he was a toddler, you know, he used the chemical substance found on the tip of match sticks to kill the then Jaffna Mayor Alfred Turayappa. You can very well imagine the amount of match sticks he must had collected to gather enough chemical to assassinate the mayor. You call such a person a coward?"

"Sorry Dhammika. I was not aware of your close relationship with him".

Cicil said sorry, and Dhammika kept quiet for some time.

Dhammika remained silent for quite some time. It seemed he was going down the memory lane.

The complete silence in the vehicle was unbearable. But, slowly each one of us fell into sleep one after the other as the vehicle sped on.

We all woke up on hearing an earth-shattering explosion. We felt our vehicle being jolted wildly.

"An airstrike on Tiger camps," Dhammika said. "There is a tunnel nearby. If we take a deviation, we can reach there fast and stay for some time."

We said okay.

"A short while ago, I was a little carried away by emotion. I am sorry," Dhammika said shyly.

"It is okay," Cicil tried to put him at ease.

The vehicle took a deviation. But this time our vehicle was not plying on the road but through an open ground.

We could see and hear fighter aircrafts scorching the skies. While our vehicle swayed from side to side as it moved on, we heard sounds of bombs being dropped and the burst of shells and later the fighters retreated.

I thought our journey would never end. No sooner than we entered a tunnel, we heard frightened cries of people.

People from the nearby villages had assembled there. They cried because they mistook our vehicles for an enemy motorcade.

When bombs and shells were being showered on villages, the people were having food inside the tunnel. When they were assured that we were not from the enemy camp, they continued with their dinner. Three youngsters were serving food under the supervision of an old man. A young man, who was engrossed in a laptop, came to us when he sighted us.

He said, "This aerial attack began early in the morning. They are bombing us thinking that there are Tiger camps here. They are targeting schools, hospitals and even huts of poor people. Anyway, if I am not mistaken, all of you are journalists. Better stay here and continue your journey when the situation improves."

Then he called a man, who was serving food, in Malayalam.

"Ikka, Ivarkkukoodi Kodukku" (Brother, please serve food to these people also.)

I couldn't suppress my curiosity. "Are you a Malayalee? What are you doing here?"

"I am Jinachandran, a Malayalee born and raised in UK. My parents are in London. After graduating from London School of Economics, I thought of studying the economic repercussions of war. I thought this was the best school to study it and came over. But now the topic has changed."

By that time, that old man came with food for us.

Jinachandran introduced him to us. "This is Ahmed Ali, the man who feeds the refugees here. You must have heard about him. He hails from Thalassery in Kannur, Kerala. He is the owner of the Malabar Cafe restaurant also."

"Jeevantha Jayakkodi had told us about you, Ali. Happy to meet you," I told him.

Ali, humbled by our praise, told me with much

respect, "You may call the others also. Let everyone have food."

All of us, including Dhammika and his aides, ate the food Ali served.

Ali said, "Son, this is all we can do to return the kindness this country showered on us. I have been living here for the past fifty years, and have earned a lot of money. I have built a house in Tellichery, married off my children to wealthy families, bought land and own buildings at my native place. I continue staying here though I sent back my family to Kerala. Most of my staff went back and set up their own hotels at Ernakulam and Kozhikode."

"Son, can you understand the kind of life we have here? Everywhere it's bombs and guns. Fighter planes bombard large areas, rockets fly over poor slums continuously, and they are being detained everywhere for grilling by the security officers. People are not allowed to move freely. The most unbearable thing is the door-to-door search for Tigers. Police and army personnel suspect the people of supporting Tigers while the guerillas force them to enlist their children in their army.

"As people cannot go out and work, they have no money, shops are closed, and even schools and hospitals remain shut. Fisher men are scared to go to sea. If we resist, the Tigers wreak revenge on us. If we succumb to the Tigers, the Lankan Army would surely arrest us and the torture that would follow is indescribably brutal. A life between the devil and the deep sea. I don't want to run away, and I have decided to live here until I breath my last." A short while later, he asked, "What made you come here dear? Tell me please."

I told him we were there to report on the issues faced by the people, and introduced to them the others in our team. Cicil mingled with the villagers and captured their words in her specam. Dhammika and his men sat glued to their phones; I was left with Ali and Jinachandran.

Sensing it to be the right opportunity, Jinachandran asked me in a tone of warning, "Is India unaware that the Sri Lankan government hiked its defence budget by 48 per cent by misleading the international community that a peaceful solution is not possible in this ethnic conflict? They will use these extra monies to revamp the military with the help of Pakistan and China. Won't this affect India? There are also many issues we are unaware of, like Sri Lanka blocking India from interfering in the Tamil issue, Pakistan and China taking advantage of the situation and expanding their presence in the island nation etc. This is what I could learn during my stay here for the last four years.

"Don't you think the bombs could also fall on the Indian shores? Warplanes are dropping bombs in the northeastern areas of Jaffna and Trincomalee. These areas are closer to towns like Rameshwaram, Madurai and Kanya Kumari in Tamil Nadu and to even places in Kerala like Thiruvananthapuram, Kochi and Kollam than to Sri Lankan capital Colombo.

"The flow of Sri Lankan refugees to India has increased as the war intensified. Yet everybody is keeping a blind eye to the issue, that may have social repercussions in Tamil Nadu and its neighbour state Kerala. I just don't understand why."

Interrupting our conversation, Dhammika shouted to us, "Air raids are over; now we can renew our journey."

We bid farewell to Ali and Jinachandran, and got into the vehicle. Darkness had begun to set in. Knowing fully well that we were going to have a troublesome journey, we pushed off to our destination.

Dhammika kept talking continuously on Sri Lankan politics. At times, he got emotional as well. He told us, “LTTE is not a guerilla outfit as you think. It has its own criminal justice system, schools and a parallel administrative set up running successfully.”

At another occasion, he spoke like an independent observer.

“Prabhakaran as well as Sri Lankan President Mahinda Rajapakse have completely withdrawn themselves from the peace process.”

A comment on Prabhakaran from Dhammika became a stick to beat him with in Cicil’s hands.

“I am asking this because you just mentioned Prabhakaran and the LTTE. If his outfit is not a terror organisation, why was Rajiv Gandhi killed? Why did they stage a coup in Maldives?”

Dhammika’s tone became serious. He said, “Madam, you don’t know anything. It was all for money; it was a ‘quotation’ for a huge amount.”

"Who gave the ‘quotation’ and for whom?”

He pretended as if he did not hear Cicil.

She did not allow him to escape.

"If you cannot reveal it, I shall ask you another question. Is this paid killings a fund-raising activity of the Tigers, who have distinct political ambitions?"

Dhammika's answer was immediate.

"Do you think with the meagre donations which the overseas Tamilians give them on the sly, they can wage a relentless war against an organised state?"

Cicil didn't stop and asked, "There is always a political option to build a nation. Don't you think resorting to criminal activities will affect the credibility of the movement and undermine the sympathy of even their supporters?"

As Cicil continued with her probing questions, Dhammika intervened, "That is a lapse on the part of Prabhakaran and his organisation."

Our amazement doubled when the security personnel at many places along the road recognised Dhammika and saluted him. On the way, he continued talking about the internal affairs of Sri Lanka.

At one stage, he spoke to us as if he was divulging a secret.

"The Sri Lankan Freedom Party and the United National Party, at each other's throats all the time, arrived at a consensus on how to resolve the ongoing ethnic problem. This was the major outcome of the meeting that took place between president Rajapakse Opposition Leader Vikramasinghe."

Even though he said all these things rather emotionally, I did not think he was bothered too much. At last when we were about to enter into a hermitage like guest house in Alamb, he said.

"We are now going to see an ideologue of Tigers, Prof. Vaidyalingam. He does not sleep in the nights, but keeps writing and speaking. Good listeners are his weakness as he doesn't get to speak to people often. So please bear with him as we have to get our things done."

A saint-like figure welcomed us when we entered the building after security checks. He greeted us with a laugh, "Come in Dhammika… I was trying to enlighten ABC on something."

It was then that I noticed him. AB Chandran, the editor of Ceylon Gazette and the son of Palakkad Ayyarath Balakrishna Menon.

Chandrettan, that was how I used to address him. He was a reputed journalist who wrote about international affairs under the pseudonym ABC. We were seeing each other after a long time; I embraced him. While I exchanged greetings with Vaidyalingam, ABC told him, "He was my favourite student."

Vaidyalingam said, "Is it so? A beloved disciple has more rights on a Guru than his own son."

At this remark, all of us laughed.

Vaidyalingam said with excitement, "Whatever may be the reasons of your visit, first take a bath, have food and rest. Thereafter we will talk. By that time, I will finish off this ABC."

We were more concerned about Sathyamma's daughters than the food and rest. They may be under the custody of the Tigers. Dhammika believed the last words of Athiran, the same was the case with us. So, we stood before him and did not move. We were just waiting for an opportunity to talk to him.

Prof Vaidyalingam was in no mood to inquire into the purpose of our visit. He continued lecturing Chandrettan. "ABC, we have been in the forefront of this struggle for the last 25 years, since 1983. It was then that the LTTE started their armed resistance movement under the leadership of Prabhakaran for the liberation of Tamil majority areas. A quarter of a century has passed, and the media are still spreading fake news that Sri Lankan government has the upper hand in this war. That dominance is a temporary phenomenon."

Vaidyalingam stopped as if he made a terrible mistake in his comments and looked at Dhammika, who knows everything. Then he changed the topic of our conversation.

"Tell me your problems. Do you think ABC's presence here will be a hindrance? You want an interview or an exclusive breaking news?"

"It is nothing of that sort," Dhammika said and told him of the purpose of our visit. After listening intently, Vaidyalingam asked:

"But why are these people interested in Sathyamma and her children?"

Dhammika replied immediately.

"Our Indian partner Valliyur Vasan, who does everything for us at the other end including our boys' training, protection, and many other things etc, needs it. We cannot ignore him."

Then, he pointed to me and explained to him of Sathyamma's connection with my family.

Prof. Vaidyalingam thought for a while and said, "We don't recruit anyone by force, we take those who volunteers. Dr Kathirvel is the person responsible for this. In case these girls are with us, and if they are willing, you can take them with you. Anyway, let me talk to Kathirvel."

He immediately went inside. I looked at ABC, who told me, "He has gone to his video phone. If professor asks, Kathirvel will oblige him."

We waited for quite long, but he did not come out. ABC said sarcastically,

"We don't know for how long the Tigers can pull on, because their situation is very bad. They are getting weakened by the day. They were in command in seven districts. Now their hold is limited to areas like Killinochi and Mullaitheevu only."

ABC was about to say something more. But, by then Prof. Vaidyalingam had returned.

"Since it is the request of our saviours Vasan and Dhammika, you may see Dr Kathirvel. But before you leave, I need to make some arrangements. For that we require some time. Please wait until then."

We had no idea, for how long we needed to wait.

Before taking a nap, I wrote in my diary.

11.58 P.M.

April 25, 2008

Friday

Prof. Vaidyalingam, so happy with having got more listeners, resumed his lecture. The topic was the relations between Sri Lankans and Tamils.

According to him, Sri Lanka was a part of Tamil Nadu once upon a time and got separated from the mainland due to some tectonic shifts and became an island. The majority of the population of the newly formed island Tamils who followed a Dravidian culture. When Buddhism was gaining popularity worldwide, a large chunk of Tamils converted to Buddhism and elevated themselves as the natives of Sri Lanka, while the others got sidelined in their own country, he said.

He shared with us another interesting information. There are two types of Tamils in Sri Lanka: Indigenous

Tamils and neo Tamils. The latter were brought to Sri Lanka by the British to work in their tea plantations.

"We consider both people as equals. But the government does not consider the Tamils as its citizens. How can the government ignore them as they played a big role in building this nation? For generations, they have been sweating it out to make the country great. How can they deny Tamil's right to live with dignity?"

"We will continue our fight until we achieve our goal of winning self-governance in regions where Tamils are a majority."

I dozed off listening to his verbal assault but woke up from my slumber when I heard somebody taking Dr Kathirvel's name.

It took a few minutes for me to understand what was happening around me. All the arrangements to take us to a secret location, where youngsters being trained to become suicide bombers are put up, to meet Dr Kathirvel had been made. Prof Vaidyalingam's aides and a special emissary would be accompanying us. If Sathyamma's daughters were there, we could bring them back. Those who came with Dhammika would remain here until we return.

When we were about to leave, Prof Vaidyalingam asked with a hint of anxiety in his voice, "Is it necessary for all of you to go there? Won't Sathyamam and Dhammika be enough?"

Dhammika intervened, "They are journalists who help us to make the world think in favour of our demand. We have to keep in mind the Norwegian interests also, and we cannot ignore their request."

Just as Dhammika completed his sentence, Professor nodded in agreement and said, "Then take ABC also along with you. He has been hanging around for an 'exclusive' for such a long time!"

Chandrettan was so happy to hear that. While watching the sun rise, someone tied a black ribbon over my eyes quite unexpectedly.

Though I panicked a little, Dhammika's reassuring words calmed me. He said, "Sorry. You have to follow certain procedures to meet Dr Kathirvel. You won't see anything from this moment, and cannot even talk until we meet him."

I came to know from the sound of movements that all of us, including Dhammika, were blind-folded. As Sathyamma was impassive and immersed in a world of her own, I didn't have an idea of her at the time.

Two people were helping me walk, and of course there would be more people to help others cope with the darkness.

Our journey began in a car, and later we were shifted to a truck. I realised we were moving through a hillside road, and that those sitting beside me were not from my group. But I was sure all members of our team were in the same truck.

The truck stopped somewhere and we were shifted to a jeep. After a rollercoaster ride along a bumpy road for some time, the jeep stopped. Thereafter, our journey was by foot. The person who held me and helped me walk in the right direction was a well-built man with strong hands.

I heard the chirping of night birds, and the ear-piercing noise of crickets. Far away, we heard the howling of wild animals. Then it was all very quiet. I could smell the forest though I couldn't see it. Also, I could hear water crashing down from a hilltop somewhere close. Water droplets continued to hit my body.

I don't know how long we walked like that. There was a complete silence all along the journey, nobody spoke a single word; not even our 'guardians'. The unnatural silence terrified me. May be, Dhammika was accustomed to these formalities. But, that was not the case with others. I was afraid for Cicil, Sathyamma and Chandrettan. As I couldn't withhold my anxiety any longer, I thought of saying something against their command. But by that time, one man held both of my legs. I did not cry out because I was numb with fear. That man, who held my foot, put one of them down on a lower step. Then the next foot. I counted eleven steps. At last, I heard a door being opened and suddenly a cool breeze enveloped me. I understood that we were in an air-conditioned room.

In no time, some body welcomed us by saying.

"Welcome to laboratory of Dr Kathirvel!"

I felt crazy on hearing a human voice after such a long time. Meanwhile, somebody removed my eye band. First, there was some kind of a blur in my eyes. When everything became clear, I looked around. All of us were there. Cicil was fixing her specam on her face. I understood that Sathyamma's eyes and mouth were covered; a tall, skinny fellow was untying the clothes from her face. The people who brought us there had disappeared.

It was a fully air-conditioned, spacious cellar room. There were so many unfamiliar machines, equipment, clocks, special kind of belts, beds etc. All of them were properly arranged and the room was spick and span. There were a few chairs arranged in a comfortable manner.

"I know each one of you. I got your pictures and conversations from Prof Vaidyalingam, who has directed me to help you fulfill your mission."

"Please feel free and be seated in a chair that you feel comfortable for you. I don't have anything special to offer you. I don't have errand boys or watchman to order them about. Even guards are posted one kilometre away from here. I and my creations. That's all we have here."

Though he talked to us in a polite and sweet manner, I noticed something wrong in his attitude towards us. His next movements confirmed my fears. When we were about to have sit, he asked abruptly, "You don't have the pictures of that boy and girls, right? You know only their names; and I don't know the name of any of them. After all, what's there in a name?"

He paused a little, laughed and continued, "Here, we have only numbers and that is the truth, the only truth.

When several people share the same names, the very idea of having a name is unreal. The future belongs to numbers, not names."

We exchanged glances at one other and managed to convey that we were in the company of a mad man.

Dr Kathirvel did not pay any attention to our discomfort and said,

"Look at that screen. You can see all those who are under my custody and their numbers. Tell me the numbers you want..."

Dr Kathirvel pressed on a remote. The image which first appeared on the screen was that of a sleeping woman; the video was being streamed live and her scroll number was three. Focussing on the rapid eye movements of the sleeping woman, he said, "She is having a beautiful dream. You know, while having a good dream, our eyelids move rapidly. We can read the anxiety experienced in the sub-conscious mind by watching the movements of the eye balls."

He stopped the narration, and asked us:

"Is this your number?"

We looked at Sathyamma. She shook her head in the negative.

Cicil held Sathymma's hand lightly, and asked her softly, "If the pictures of your daughters appear, do tell us".

The next picture numbered seven appeared on the screen where a teenage girl was tossing and turning in the bed as she could not sleep. Her clothes were out of place.

When the pictures of women corresponding to numbers 11, 17, 22 were shown, Sathyamma was seen watching them with rapt attention. Another 63 videos were screened on after the other. But the daughters Sathyamma was searching for were not among them.

"Now I will take you into the bedrooms of our male inmates." He showed about three hundred photos of boys and young men on the screen.

Sathyamma shouted, "No, I don't want to see any of them."

We were stunned. This mother wanted only her daughters. Did she not pine for her son?

In order to pacify us, Cicil said, "Leave it. She hates her son that viscerally. God alone knows why."

On thinking of what Athiran told us about Sivarathnam, we decided to leave it at that. It would be a waste of time looking for his picture.

Dr Kathirvel switched off the projector and said, "These 63 girls and 107 boys, whom you refused to see, are all the people I have with me right now."

Dhammika, who was silent till then, intervened and said, "We are in fact looking for the girls who were brought back to this place very recently."

Dr Kathirvel's reaction was immediate, "Most of the faces look similar, aren't they? So, I don't remember anybody's face in particular."

An impatient Dhammika looked at us and asked him, "In the recent past, have you brought back any girls who ran away from here?"

"Oh Yes, yes," Dr Kathirvel said immediately. "A total of 11 persons; all of them cooperated with my suggestions completely and gave me the best of results. All those bravehearts have successfully completed their missions as well."

"Can we see them?"

Cicil, I and Dhamika asked in unison.

"You want to see them or their performances?" Dr Kathirvel asked us excitedly.

"They were my creations. Only when others

appreciate their performances, I will have the satisfaction of being their creator."

I thought he was begging for recognition and appreciation of his works. The entreaties of the lunatic were hideous to watch. Whatever may be the truth, we have to see the girls, dead or alive. Cicil, who had something else also in her mind, joined me in giving him the go ahead.

"We will watch it."

Dr Kathirvel jumped like a child, eager to show off his new toy to a buddy, from his chair.

"Okay. Then, you first watch my all-time best 3 and judge me after that."

He invited us to look at the screen.

We looked at the screen with anxiety.

An image of a woman walking on a busy street appeared on the screen.

"Oh, Saroja dearest..." Sathyamma screamed at the top of her voice; meanwhile, the woman exploded on the screen as we sat bewildered.

Dr Kathirvel was wildly clapping, while Sathyamma,

not knowing what had happened, blabbered incoherently. "My daughter … My sweet child..."

Dr Kathirvel was totally indifferent to her plight and shouted with excitement, "Take a look. Just look at that..."

Another girl was running towards a convoy of vehicles. No sooner her closeup was on the screen, Sathyamma screamed aloud, "Savithri, my dear daughter!" Her screams rose to a crescendo and tapered off; by then, the girl jumped on to one of the vehicles and set off the bomb and the vehicle burst into flames.

"See that. What an achievement!"

Dr.Kathirvel was paying no attention to us at all. He was glued to the screen, and he kept clapping with joy, all by himself. He requested us to watch the next video.

A woman walked into a highly protected office complex. A long shot. In the next shot, she was seen sitting in an office room. Then her closeup- she was talking to a man rather mechanically.

Sathyamma let out a loud, long cry: "Sathyawathi, my daughter…" She also exploded along with the entire office and the men and material around. A huge ball of fire appeared on the screen.

"It is not over. Look at that!" He was very happy, uncontrollably excited and was jumping about the place.

"Stop it!" The terrifying roar came from an unexpected quarter. It was Dhammika.

"This is their mother," he was trembling in anger.

"Is that so?" Dr Kathirvel accepted Dhammika's outburst as a mark of appreciation.

"Brave Woman!" He looked at Sathyamma and showered praises on her. "I salute you mother. You gave me your daughters to obey my suggestions for the success of my mission. I am grateful to you for your appreciation and for witnessing their amazing bravery."

He bowed his head before Sathyamma with the graceful steps of a dancer. All of a sudden Sathyamma caught hold of his overcoat, and shouted at his face like a wounded lioness.

"Fix a bomb like that in my body, can you?"

At this time, Dr Kathirvel began dancing like a maniac. Pushing Sathyamma away, he walked in a weird rhythm and went to a chamber at the foot of the screen. He fished out a thick belt and showed it to Sathyamma.

"Look here old lady! You are no longer young enough to wear this belt, or to operate it." He touched the buckle of the belt and said, "Only when you press this buckle switch, the bomb goes off and you don't have the guts to do that. I am very sorry. You just cannot do that. You are too old to do that."

He put the belt on his shoulder and said, "To blast oneself into pieces, you have to accept the suggestion whole-heartedly. One needs extraordinary emotional strength to do that. Only immature minds can be swayed and strengthened by suggestions. They accept the suggestions and execute whatever their masters command. That's why I target youngsters; they can be remotely-controlled without any fuss, you know".

Before he could complete his words, Sathyamma lunged forward and snatched the belt from his shoulder and tried desperately to tie it to herself. When she realised she could not do that, she ran outside with the belt. We ran after her without thinking of the consequences. Earlier when we were brought there blind-folded, we had no idea of the topography of the area. When we were running behind Sathyamma, we came to know that the spacious interiors were carved out of a massive rock.

We were awe-struck at the strength and courage displayed by Sathymma, who had sat tired and impassive throughout the journey. Now, she was trying very hard not to get caught and to reach Dr Kathirvel somehow.

The entire rock was defended by a barbed wire fence. One can escape the place only through a secret passage. May be, we were brought in yesterday through that secret path. Not having seen any exit point Sathyamma was running around the rock, and when she felt she would be caught for sure, she tried to climb the rock with all her strength. All of us began climbing the rock; Cicil was the first to climb after her, followed by Dhammika and me.

I looked back. ABC had started climbing up. Dr Kathirvel stood below, clapping his hands in joy as if he was watching a sports event. As all his security guards were far away, they had no idea what was going on at the lab.

Giving no chance to Cicil to catch up with her, Sathyamma reached the top of the rock and put on the belt. She then turned and told Cicil. "Clear out, all of you... With this belt I want to embrace him and finish him forever. There should never be a suicide bomber like my unfortunate girls!"

Cicil objected. "Don't do that Sathyamma! Not just him, even you and may be, all of us would be killed."

During this time, Cicil was climbing the rock cleverly to reach Sathyamma. Dr Kathirvel shouted from below, "Just wearing the belt won't do. The switch is on its buckle. Press it. Make it fast!"

While Sathyamma bent a little to look for the buckle, Cicil caught her tightly with both her hands. Tried to stop her hands. They wrestled and both of them fell down on the rock. Cicil somehow managed to snatch the belt from Sathyamma and threw it away. Dr Kathirvel cried out in exasperation, "You let me down. What a disappointment!"

On hearing this, Sathyamma rushed towards him and jumped down; fortunately, Cicil could catch Sathyamma by one of her hands. She hanged in the air on Cicil's outstretched hand and tried to catch Cicil with her other hand, may be due to the fear of death which emerged all of a sudden. In a moment, she frantically tried to pull up and catch Cicil's free hand and caught the platinum chain she was wearing, in which the specam was attached. The chain broke and the goggles fell off.

Cicil watched her goggles falling on the stairs beneath the rock and breaking into a thousand pieces in stunned silence. Even then, Sathyamma was hanging from one of her hands. Soon, Dhammika and Chandran arrived and pulled Sathyamma to safety.

Meanwhile, the security guards arrived on the orders of Dr Kathirvel, who didn't hide his disappointment and ordered them:

"Take them away, bloody mood-spoilers..."

We were taken out of the forest in the same fashion in which we were brought there. Prof Vaidyalingam had gone to Mullatheevu urgently to attend the funeral of seventeen Tigers who were killed in an airstrike at Chemmalai on the 11 April. So, we needed not to wait for him. We dropped ABC there.

On our return, we made Sathyamma sit with Dhammika in a vehicle, while I and Cicil followed it in another.

The moment the vehicle began to move, Cicil put her head on my shoulder and began crying:

"I have failed... I have failed..."

At the moment, I did not understand what she had meant. She was sobbing inconsolably.

"This is my last official journey as a professional journalist…"

As I sat confused, she continued between her sobs, "One week, and almost 140 hours. Whatever I have heard and seen in these unforgettable hours are gone in a second! My specam which recorded all that must have cursed me for ignoring it and shifting my focus to save a life. Every fragment of the cam must be angry with me for this."

Then only I realised it: all that she had recorded in her specam had been lost irrecoverably during her attempt to rescue Sathyamma. How could she bear it? I felt her pain. Still, I tried my best to console her.

"Remember, it happened while you tried to save a life. Had you not done that, you know what would have happened. Sathyamma would have detonated herself and killed all of us including Dr Kathirvel. Who knows?"

She lifted her head from my shoulder and looked at me. She said, "That should have happened. And, that too should have been captured by my specam. A very rare exclusive!"

She leaned on my shoulder again and said with palpable disappointment.

"A journalist should be a journalist from the very beginning to the end and nothing else. I forgot that basic lesson here. That small mistake on my part destroyed everything. Just think of the things I could not show the world due to that single lapse! From the exodus of innocent people seeking refuge in distant shores to their brutal massacre in the sea, and to the creation of human bombs by a demon called Kathirvel..."

She sobbed again. "I am defeated, I don't deserve a life as a journalist any longer. Journalist Cicil Glancer is no more. She has committed suicide."

She went on muttering these words despite my sincere efforts to console her. Sometime later, she said, "I have one more thing to do. I want to take Sathyamma, who has nobody now, to India. I want to hand her over to the Jesuit Refugee Home in Munnamsathiram. If at any stage, her son takes her home, let that be. Or else, let her live on the shore, looking at the sea and wait for her daughters hoping that they would come out of their eternal sleep in Lanka one fine day and run into her arms."

When we reached the private guest house of Dhammika, it was late at night. Cicil wanted to go back to India that night itself. We extended thanks to Dhammika for his excellent hospitality, protection, care and love. As we stepped into the boat of Twan Rabeer to return to the Indian shore, Cicil was still in tears. Sathyamma stood beside her like a machine which had stopped in its tracks.

We don't know at what time we reached Chinnatheevu and got into Vasan's boat. Vasan was not to be seen, but the boat driver was the same guy-Saravanan.

Cicil and I sat in the same seat. Sathyamma was in the other seat leaning on to her long stick. As the boat moved, I was feeling sleepy.

Before I succumbed to sleep, I noted in my diary. 11.59 P.M.

April 26, 2008

Saturday

A flaming water column rose before my closed eyes! Originating from the depths of the sea and sweeping aside the waves, it produces countless droplets of water under the limitless sky. Beneath those spherical particles, the silhouette of a tall and muscular man emerges. There is a sword in his right hand; the index finger of his left hand is pointing at someone. In a flash, that sword rises in the sky and comes down with tremendous power... I was stunned. Suddenly I got back to my senses, and opened my eyes.

Wasn't it the same dream I had repeatedly had just a week earlier?

A relentless scream brought me back to my senses. Cicil was pointing to the floor of the boat and I saw

Saravanan lying dead in a pool of blood, with his head severed. Next to him was Sathyamma, with a sword, unsheathed from her walking stick, in her right hand and her left hand pointed towards Saravana's severed head.

She roared, "That is him, Sivarathnam! I am ashamed to say he was my son."

A drop of blood rolled down the tip of the sword and it tried to seek refuge in Sathyamma's clenched fist. She shook it off her hand and said,

"A man of justice called Sathyavageeshwaran had presented this sword to my father long ago. My dad had treasured it as a sacred weapon. Later, he handed it over to me and said, 'Let this sword be your protector'. The moment it touched this wretch, it has become impure. By using it on such an unscrupulous person, I have also become impure."

For a moment, she looked at us with eyes full with gratitude and said, "This sea purifies everything."

She didn't wait any further and to the shock of all of us, jumped into the sea. Despite the emotional upheaval, we collected ourselves and rushed to the spot where she jumped. There was a flaming water column where

Sathyamma disappeared. It came down from the infinite expanses of the sky, parted the waves and went deep down into the sea.

Then the time was...

I have no idea.

It had been a long time since it stopped working.

■